Original title:
Rooted in Reflection

Copyright © 2025 Creative Arts Management OÜ
All rights reserved.

Author: Arabella Whitmore
ISBN HARDBACK: 978-1-80567-315-6
ISBN PAPERBACK: 978-1-80567-614-0

In the Cradle of Remembrance

In a garden of thoughts, I often roam,
Digging up dreams, like weeds, from my home.
My past likes to play tag under the sun,
Tripping on memories, oh what fun!

I ponder the days when my hair was so bright,
Now it's a mix — oh, what a sight!
I tried to recall all my dance moves so sweet,
But ended up looking just like two left feet.

Once I was daring, with stories to tell,
Now my boldest feat is how to brew tea well.
I laugh at my selfie from a decade ago,
Was that really me, or just a shadow?

In the attic of laughter, I gather my cheer,
With echoes of giggles that tickle my ear.
So I toast all the follies of youth gone astray,
And wink at the future, come what may!

When Silence Speaks Volumes

In a room full of chatter, I sat very still,
Listening to whispers, they gave me a thrill.
Thoughts danced like shadows, quick on their feet,
My mind played charades, a whimsical feat.

The walls were all giggles, the floor a wise sage,
My tongue had a party, but I missed the stage.
While silence was crafting a symphony near,
I lost track of days, but gained a good cheer.

Classics of the Inner Dialogue

Oh, the battles I fight with the voices inside,
They argue like siblings, and rarely decide.
One says I'm a genius, the other, a fool,
At least they agree that I'm breaking the rule.

With thoughts like popcorn, they pop and they scatter,
My brain's a circus, with acrobats that chatter.
Should I wear the red shoes or go with the blue?
Maybe I'll ask them, but who, and to who?

Beneath the Veil of Experience

I once wore a hat made of lessons and yarn,
Each thread held a story, some sweet, some a scorn.
The brim was adorned with my past's little quirks,
A parade of mishaps, oh how life often jerks!

Beneath all that fabric, a wisdom so vast,
Life flicked me a wink, said, "Hey, make it last!"
So I wear my experiences like jewels on my chest,
Though some days I feel they're a bit more than zest.

The Essence of What Remains

In the attic of memories, dust bunnies waltz,
They dance with old dreams, no need for a pulse.
Each trinket I kept has a tale of its own,
I laugh at the treasures I've collected and grown.

A broken clock whispers, 'I used to tick on,'
Now it's a paperweight, my sanity's con.
Yet, as I sift through the chaos and mess,
I find gems of laughter that I must confess.

Musing Where Remembrance Blooms

In dusty nooks, my thoughts take flight,
Like socks that vanish, it's quite the sight.
A memory jog, a mental race,
Forget the coffee, find my misplaced vase.

Nostalgic visions swirl like cheese,
Why do old jokes always seem to tease?
I laugh at moments, silly and bright,
As echoes twirl in the fading light.

In the Quiet Corners of Memory

There's a place where giggles often rest,
A comedic nook, in my mind's chest.
I ponder on dinners that went awry,
And wonder just when did the veggies cry?

Like lost remotes, memories sneak peek,
In corners where they play hide and seek.
Who needs a plan when chaos reigns?
My thoughts grow wild with comedic pains.

The Art of Looking Inward

Self-expectations are jokes gone too far,
Like trying to fit into a child's car.
I chuckle at dreams that seem so absurd,
Like a cat who claims it can fly like a bird.

So I dive deep into my tangled mind,
Where wisdom swims, and laughter's aligned.
It's art, indeed, this funny charade,
Discovering wisdom where folly is made.

The Dialogue of Heart and Mind

My heart says bake, my mind says nap,
The negotiation's absurd—a comedy tap!
Should I dance, or should I just sit and stare?
The mental tug-of-war gets too rarefied air.

With each decision, a chuckle is shared,
Logic vs. whimsy, a duel well-prepared.
I smile at the banter, a theatrical play,
Who knew my thoughts could be so droll in sway?

Moments of Stillness

In the yard, I found a shoe,
Wondered how it got there too.
It's not a path I often tread,
Perhaps a squirrel's lost thread!

Amid the weeds, a garden gnome,
Convinced it's trying to find home.
I laughed so hard, the neighbors peered,
What's so funny? Oh, my dear!

Reflections on Hidden Paths

Treading softly on a walk,
Nature's whispers start to talk.
A bee buzzed by, did a twist,
Then crashed right into a flower fist!

With each step, a giggle grows,
Even the wind begins to pose.
Through paths unseen, I stumbled around,
Life's light humor is profound!

Secrets Cradled in Quiet

Oh, the secrets trees might tell,
Of how they grew and where they fell.
A squirrel made a cozy nest,
While I sit pondering, quite obsessed!

Leaves flutter down, an acorn drops,
Who knew nature had such flops?
Sipping tea, I watch the scene,
Laughter in moments unforeseen!

The Solace of the Soul's Garden

In my garden, weeds do waltz,
With daisies dressed in their faults.
The sun smiles wide and cats do prance,
Even fungi join in the dance!

Pondering life amidst the blooms,
I spot a frog claiming rooms.
"Is this your throne?" I tease the chap,
He croaks a laugh, then takes a nap!

Shards of Meaning

In the garden of thought, I trip and fall,
Stumbling on wisdom that's barely tall.
With each funny thought, I giggle and grin,
Like a fish in a state of attempting to swim.

Jokes sprout like weeds, and laughter does bloom,
In the corners of my cluttered room.
Chasing tiny truths like a dog with a bone,
Only to find them—sometimes I'm alone.

Echoing Heartbeats

My heart plays the drums, a comedic beat,
While my thoughts do a dance, interrupted by feet.
Each heartbeat a joke, a kick in the air,
Echoing loudly like I just don't care.

Chuckle and snicker, life's not so grim,
As echoes ricochet and laughter starts to brim.
Is that a punchline? Or just my old shoe?
Either way, I'm chuckling—how about you?

Ever-Green Discernment

Wisdom like grass, so green yet so sly,
It tickles my toes when I pass it by.
Each blade a reminder, a wink in the sun,
Saying, 'Hey buddy, isn't this fun?'

Underneath the trees, shade pops up to tease,
'Let's contemplate life over a cool breeze.'
Yet laughter's the tune that I hear on repeat,
Dance with the leaves, let's skip down the street!

The Language of Shadows

Shadows whisper secrets in a giggly tone,
Like the plots of a sitcom that's all on its own.
Dancing around corners, they lead the way,
With punchlines that often have nothing to say.

Catch me if you can, said the shadow to me,
I'll hide in the corners, that's where I'll be.
In the light of the day, I'll blend, I'll play tricks,
Just don't take me seriously, I'm just full of kicks!

In the Embrace of Solumn Stillness

In quiet corners, thoughts do swirl,
The cat's judging me, in a tiny curl.
Standing still now, I ponder my shoe,
Did I really mean to bake that stew?

The clock's ticking loud, shouting my name,
In solitude's grasp, it's all just a game.
I laugh at my past, the puns that I've made,
Like the time I wore slippers on date night parade!

A mirror reflects the chaos I've sown,
With hair that's a mess and socks that have grown.
This moment feels grand, like I'm on a spree,
But really I'm just fending off monotony.

So in stillness, I chuckle at my plight,
A jester in rituals, holding on tight.
Every pause a punchline, every breath a jest,
In this quiet embrace, I'm simply the best!

Language of the Unseen

Whispers of socks, lost in the gloom,
They've formed a rebellion, plotting their doom.
A spatula's dreams of flipping a cake,
While fruit flies conspire, oh the mess they will make!

Invisible friends join the kitchen's delight,
Measuring cups laugh at my cooking plight.
The blender hums loudly, it's quite a debate,
Whisking up tales of my unfortunate fate.

I chat with the toaster, sharing our woes,
It pops up crumbs, but nobody knows.
With a wink from the fridge, we dance in the night,
In the language of silence, everything's right.

Hidden voices, a chorus unseen,
Making my kitchen a comedic scene.
These kitchens of humor where laughter will stream,
Sparked by the chaos of my culinary dream!

Revisiting Forgotten Landscapes

Through scribbled notes, I travel back,
To landscapes of laughter and a few things I lack.
The playground's a jungle, daring me still,
But I trip on my shoelace, oh what a thrill!

Replaying old jokes that once made me grin,
Like the time I was chased by a goofy kin.
The swings creak with stories of summers long past,
While the slide shows my speed in a moment so fast.

A bicycle ride turns into a feat,
With training wheels on, I'm easy to beat.
Yet the thrill of the race against my old foes,
Leaves me laughing aloud as my confidence grows.

These landscapes of memory, laughing with pride,
In the echoes of childhood, I'll freely abide.
Each stumble a story, each fall a delight,
As I wander through mirth on this whimsical night!

When the Heart Remembers

In the attic of heart, memories dance,
Some wear silly hats, while others wear pants.
A birthday gone wrong with a cake that was sad,
And a unicycle ride that turned out just bad!

Tales of the past bring chuckles anew,
Like the tears from that onion I chose to pursue.
A flipside of laughter, a soft fleeting sigh,
When I mix up my dates, oh my, oh my!

Each grin from the past strikes joy like a dart,
Revisiting moments that warmed up my heart.
These heartstrings play melodies, silly and sweet,
Where the laughter flows free, no reason to cheat.

With each fleeting thought, I burst into glee,
For remembering's fun, just like a sweet spree.
So here's to the heart that chuckles and gleams,
In laughter we wander, living our dreams!

Whispers of a Still Mind

In silence, my thoughts take a jog,
Chasing after a very lost fog.
They tumble and bounce like a rubber ball,
Falling flat – oh, what a great brawl.

A duck passes by, quacking in rhyme,
Its words are so wise – just wasting time.
I ponder this cosmic, noodle-like quest,
Wondering if I'm really the best!

Plans of grandeur, they dance in my brain,
Yet somehow they all go down the drain.
Like socks in the wash, they vanish in air,
And I giggle, forgetting my care.

So here I sit, with laughter and cheer,
A still mind's a playground – what fun is here.
As thoughts do the tango and trees sway alongside,
Life's joke is delightful, with humor as guide.

Echoes of the Past

I met my old self in a vintage store,
He whispered secrets from days of yore.
With bows in his hair and mismatched socks,
He giggled at time like a tick-tocking box.

Memories drift like leaves on the ground,
Some funny, some silly, in laughter they drown.
A wild game of tag with the years on the run,
Just trying to catch up, but oh! Ain't it fun?

Photos in frames with questionable styles,
And hairstyles that bring back the best wacky miles.
I laugh at the choices, the fads that we wore,
The ghost of past me couldn't take anymore.

In echoes of laughter, we dance through the years,
With inside jokes turning into our cheers.
So here's to the moments, the quirky and vast,
As I high-five my shadow, and grin at my past.

Beneath the Surface

A pond reflects the frogs having fun,
With capes made of lily pads — they're all on the run.
Diving below, they're holding a party,
Splashing around – the vibe is so hearty.

Bubbles chatter with glee in the dark,
Where fish play charades, a swim and a lark.
They giggle and swish, like they just won a prize,
Underwater antics, a spectacle to rise.

Seashells gossip about who came to play,
While rocks pull up chairs for the midday ballet.
With currents that tickle and sand that delights,
My laugh echoes upward, a calming sight.

So here in my bubble, I see all the cheer,
As aquatic life shows how to live without fear.
Each ripple a tickle, a moment to treasure,
Underneath the surface, pure joy beyond measure.

Shadows of Solitude

In the corner, my shadow's a joker,
Making faces, pretending it's sober.
It winks ever slyly as the light bends,
Silly antics from my own little friend.

Loneliness sings like a badly-tuned song,
But my shadow just dances, it knows it belongs.
It flails at the wall with a grand faux pas,
Creating a spectacle, what a quirky czar!

Together we ponder the world's wacky plight,
While shadows parade in the soft moonlight.
In silence, we giggle at the things we can't say,
Making wise cracks while the world slips away.

So here we bask in our silliness shown,
For solitude's laughter can never be alone.
When shadows are playful, and worries grow dim,
Life's a circus and we're both in on a whim.

Harvesting Shadows of the Past

In the garden of my mind,
Ghosts of laughter intertwine.
I trip on memories, oh what fun,
Chasing rays from the fading sun.

Silly thoughts grow like weeds,
Planting jokes, pulling breeds.
A mishmash of blunders, a vibrant mix,
Like my aunt's hat—what a fix!

Petty squabbles, old debates,
Resurface like granddad's plates.
Digging up tales, wearing a grin,
Who knew a past could brew such din?

So here I stand, with shadows in tow,
Poking at memories like a curious crow.
Harvesting laughter, with a wink and a jest,
In this patch of nostalgia, I feel truly blessed.

The Stillness Between the Leaves

In the silence where squirrels play,
A dance of shadows leads astray.
Whispers of the wind, a soft applause,
Twirling tales without a cause.

Leaves converse in hushed tones,
Teasing branches with silly moans.
Nature's gossip, such a spree,
I swear I heard it mention me!

Each crunch beneath my toes
Is a secret only nature knows.
With every pause, a giggle found,
As I listen closely, I hear the sound.

In this hush, a comic guise,
Nature's humor never lies.
A stillness ripe with quirky wit,
Amidst the leaves, I choose to sit.

Woven Threads of Yesterday

With stitches of laughter, I mend the seams,
Twisting tales, crafting dreams.
Old yarn balls tangle in my mind,
Knots of joy that always unwind.

I pull at threads, the colorful past,
Each one unique, some hold fast.
Whimsical patterns from each time spent,
An odd tapestry in my basement dent.

With scissors in hand, I snip away
At those cringe-worthy moments—hey hey!—
What a quilt of blunders, pure delight,
Crafted in the glow of the moonlight.

So here's to laughter, this fabric of days,
Woven together in peculiar ways.
Each thread a memory, each knot a jest,
My quilt of yesterday is simply the best!

In the Shade of Self-Discovery

Beneath a tree, I sit and ponder,
With thoughts that flit and occasionally wander.
Shadows stretch, like my wild ideas,
Making me chuckle, oh how it clears!

The roots below, they tickle my toes,
With every giggle, the wisdom grows.
Branches above wave at my plight,
"Come play with us, you funny sight!"

Conversations with bark, oh what a treat,
They crack the codename of my next feat.
In this shade, my laughter blooms,
Like wildflowers in mischievous rooms.

Unraveling secrets with whimsical flair,
Found in the shade of this gentle care.
Self-discovery's not so dire,
When you can laugh and light the fire!

The Corners of the Mind's Eye

In corners where the thoughts play,
A sock debates with yesterday.
The cat is plotting world domination,
While I just seek a vacation.

A burger dances on my screen,
With fries that wear a golden sheen.
I laugh at dreams of flying high,
Then trip on thoughts of pie in the sky.

A memory pops, then slips away,
Like soap in a bathtub, it won't stay.
I ponder deep, then quickly swerve,
It's hard to think when you lose your nerve.

Amidst this chaos, I find a way,
To chuckle at the games I play.
In mind's eye corners, laughter blooms,
While socks and cats take up their rooms.

Fleeting Thoughts on Still Waters

Thoughts like bubbles are afloat,
Some drift by in a silly boat.
A fish in glasses gazes back,
While ducks debate, 'What's on the snack?'

The pond reflects my frowning face,
It seems to chuckle at my pace.
'Take a break!' it gently quips,
As I do mental backflips.

Fleeting ideas swim around,
A poet's block, they have just found.
I try to catch them with a net,
But end up splashing—what a threat!

In this watery theater, oh so clear,
A giggle bubbles up to hear.
With every splash, my worries sink,
Time's a puddle—with no time to think.

Beneath the Surface of Awareness

Beneath the surface, thoughts do spin,
Like a hamster wheel that's just kicked in.
A sock is missing, wait—what's that?
A dance-off, led by my pet cat.

The fridge hums a wobbly tune,
It dreams of food—a midnight swoon.
I laugh at cheese that rolls away,
And join its frolic, hip-hip-hooray!

Layers of thought, in tangled heaps,
While wisdom snores and dreamily sleeps.
I try to search these winding roads,
Yet find more socks—forgotten loads.

In this deep dive of woeful bliss,
I open the door to silly, with a twist.
Awareness, oh how we all stray,
But laughter keeps the doubts at bay.

Serenity in Retrospect

I glance back on today's slight chaos,
Waving at the socks, like a circus rhinos.
A coffee spill, a playful cat,
No one told me life served like that!

In retrospect, a trip on a shoe,
A turtle's race—oh, to be blue.
I ponder the wisdom that I've accrued,
While mixing up my lunch with food.

Serenity comes in bursts of giggles,
With wisdom dancing then doing jigs.
Each quirky moment, a canvas splashed,
Life's delightful mess, forever dashed.

With laughter echoing in my chest,
I realize that I'm truly blessed.
In these stories, so jumbled and bright,
Serenity reigns in the joy of the night.

Inward Journeys

I took a trip inside my head,
Found a sandwich, stale as bread.
With each thought, my brain did flip,
Wondering if I left the stove on - oh drip!

In this maze where echoes dwell,
I argue with a ghost named Mel.
She tells me jokes, but they fall flat,
Like a cat who thinks it's a circus acrobat.

Who knew my mind was such a place,
With a mirror ball and a funny face?
I danced around my tangled schemes,
Waking up to laugh all my waking dreams.

So here I stand, a traveler bold,
In this carnival of mind, uncontrolled.
Taking rides on thoughts that swoop,
While munching popcorn from my own mental troop.

The Depths Within

Diving deep into my own abyss,
I found my lunchbox, what a twist of bliss.
A lost sock waved back in cheer,
As I swam through memories, bold and clear.

Down below, I met a wise old fish,
Said, 'Life's full of quirks; that's my only wish.'
We swapped stories like old-time pals,
While searching for misplaced jelly jars and gals.

Philosophy bubbles, like soap in a bath,
Tickling my toes, making me laugh.
I pondered why grass is always greener,
As my brain did a waltz, less than a screener.

Emerging up, what a sight to see,
Came the laughter and giggles—oh, joyful glee!
The depths within are quite absurd,
But they serve a feast of laughter, undeterred.

Threads of Introspection

I took a thread and pulled it tight,
Unraveled stories in the night.
Each stitch held secrets, funny and quaint,
Like trying to dance without a paint.

Through the fabric of my wandering mind,
Lies a quilt of quirks, one of a kind.
Patchwork memories of slip and trip,
With occasional dips and an ice-cream flip.

Stitch by stitch, the plot unfolds,
Knitting laughter in my heart that holds.
Who knew reflection could be a giggle spree,
With a sneeze of joy and a hiccup of glee?

So grab a needle, come join the fun,
In laughter's threads, we've only begun.
Turn your frown into a cartoonish grin,
As we patch together, where thoughts spin.

Unraveled Thoughts

I sat and pondered—what a mess,
My thoughts unravelled in a fancy dress.
One cat danced while the others sat,
While I tried to sort this strange format.

A noodle got knotted, just like my brain,
As I tried to remember—was it sunshine or rain?
Then came a wave of nonsense galore,
Like trying to juggle while balancing a snore.

Each ponder, a rollercoaster ride,
With loops and curls that I can't hide.
Wacky ideas, both big and small,
Like a giraffe trying to do the limbo at all.

In every loop, a chuckle I find,
As my thoughts unravel, oh, how unconfined!
So let's toast to this humorous maze,
Where laughter and folly are the best praise!

The Weight of Stillness

In the chair, I sat so proud,
Thoughts like clouds, they billowed loud.
But when I tried to move a toe,
My brain forgot, much to my woe.

A spider's web began to sway,
I pondered life in disarray.
What's heavier, a thought or dream?
Turns out it's just my lunch, it seems!

Sipping coffee, I drift away,
While the clock ticks hours in dismay.
A nap feels like a noble quest,
But then I wake, still in the vestibule's nest.

So, I embrace this gentle fight,
Being still is quite the plight.
Who knew the weight could be so grand?
I'll blame my thoughts, and not my hand!

Growing Through Silence

In the garden, flowers sleep tight,
But weeds pop up, giving me fright.
I talk to plants, but they just blink,
Are they shy, or just a bit pink?

The tomatoes don't respond at all,
Laughing at me, they seem to sprawl.
I think they're plotting, oh what a game,
Next spring, I'll finally stake my claim.

When silence reigns, I start to hum,
But bees stop by, and I feel dumb.
"Is this a concert?" I ask in glee,
Their buzzing says, "Just let us be!"

Yet through this calm, I might just find,
A fruit of laughter, sweet and kind.
Next year's blooms, I'll give a show,
Perhaps a dance with plants in tow!

In Search of Forgotten Dreams

In a box under my bed it lies,
A dream of heights and distant skies.
I pull it out, it's dusty, oh dear!
Did I forget it or was it just fear?

An elephant in a tutu waits,
I chuckle loud; this stuff creates.
Why did I dream of this odd sight?
Oh wait, it's still a pretty light bite!

Floating castles and a cat that sings,
A chorus of laughter, what joy it brings!
But as I ponder, the clock ticks on,
Should I wake dreams or just move along?

With a wink and a grin, I take flight,
Through swirling thoughts till the moon's in sight.
Each forgotten whim, a treasure, it seems,
Now I'll soar—funny things are my dreams!

Reveries Underneath the Surface

In the pond, my thoughts take a swim,
Frogs croak loudly, becoming quite dim.
"Is this deep?" I ponder with glee,
But the fish just laugh; they're too fishy to see.

I dive down deep, what do I find?
A rubber duck, perfectly aligned.
"Is this how you think?" I yell to the sky,
The duck only quacks, not a reply!

Bubbles rise like hopes from the deep,
But all I catch are some dreams I keep.
What if I float all day with a grin—
Maybe life's best when you just dive in?

So with a splash and a wink of delight,
I rise to the surface, not giving up the fight.
Underneath it all, there's laughter to hear,
In this silly pond, life's a cheer!

The Depths of Uncharted Reflection

In a pond of my thoughts, I sit with a grin,
While pondering all the places I've been.
The ducks float by, quacking quite loud,
I'm laughing to self, this pond's like a crowd.

With every splash, a memory pops,
Of all the lost socks and shopping mall stops.
I might be a mess, that's quite clear to see,
But hey, it's all water, just let it be!

My thoughts sometimes swirl, a whirlpool of jest,
Like pasta in water, I must say, I'm blessed.
So I'll float on this boat made of words and pure glee,
Until the next wave comes to carry me free.

Reflection's a circus, with clowns and their tricks,
In a funhouse of mirrors, I gather my kicks.
With a wink and a nod, I'll dance with my fate,
In the depths of the pond, oh what a fine state!

Memories Flowing Like Streams

I sat by a stream, with thoughts all amiss,
Wondering why I can't find where it is.
With branches that wiggle, like fingers in air,
I chuckle at nature's unplanned affair.

The fish swim by, in their glittery suits,
And here I am, pondering my old school boots.
Did I really wear those? Oh, what a delight!
Let's toss them in for a fashionable fight!

The water is cool, and I feel quite alive,
As the current flows past, I watch salmon dive.
Each splash brings a giggle, a memory to seize,
Like when I tripped over a swarm of bees.

These streams of the past, they ripple and tease,
With laughter like bubbles, they float on the breeze.
A dance of the water, with me in the midst,
Oh, what a funny tale, who could resist?

In the Silence, Truth Grows

In the hush of the night, I ponder alone,
While my thoughts are as loud as my dog's silly groan.
The moon winks at me, with a sparkle and jest,
As I muse about life and give quiet a rest.

With stars as my audience, I toss out my fears,
And laugh at old worries that slipped through the years.
There's wisdom in silence, or so folks do say,
But silence just snickers and runs far away.

The crickets join in on this whimsical plight,
Their chirps turn to giggles as they echo the night.
So I sit here and chuckle, with truth in the breeze,
For funny reflections put my mind at ease.

The stillness is magic, like candy for thought,
Where jokes become wisdom, and laughter's the plot.
In the hush, I find joy, in jest I find grace,
And humor grows bright, like a smile on my face!

The Language of Contemplation

In grand conversations with thoughts in my head,
I wonder if cowbells could teach me instead.
Oh, wisdom's a hoot when it rides on a breeze,
But give me a cowbell and watch as I sneeze!

With thoughts like a melody, dancing in line,
I ponder on issues, big, small, and just fine.
The tickle of humor fits snug like a glove,
As the language of pondering turns laugh into love.

I chatter with shadows, those sneaky old blokes,
Who giggle and whisper and play all the jokes.
What fun to converse with the echoes of me,
A dialogue rich as a cup of hot tea!

So here's to the laughter, the jest we all share,
In the language of thought, there's humor in air.
Contemplation is silly, I'm learning it's true,
With each chuckle and grin, I discover what's new!

Light Filtering Through Memory's Leaves

A squirrel stole my sandwich today,
While I searched for some wisdom to say.
Memories danced like leaves in a breeze,
I laughed so hard, I fell to my knees.

Old photos cringe at my awkward pose,
My hair had styles nobody knows.
I pondered deeply, what was the fuss?
Yet I still cherish those days with a plus.

Each memory flickers, like candles aglow,
They light up the path where old laughter flows.
I poke fun at the past and its quirks,
For every big dream, there were silly perks.

So here's to the joy that life spins around,
With laughter as roots in the soil underground.
In the garden of thoughts where my chuckles gleam,
I root for the funny; it reigns supreme.

The Mosaic of Inner Landscapes

My mind's an abstract Picasso, I swear,
With colors beyond what you scholars declare.
Each stroke tells a tale, some funny, some odd,
With a laugh that weaves through, like a plump little frog.

I trip over thoughts like they're scattered stones,
A jigsaw of memories mixed with my tones.
There's a cat in a hat, and a fish with a tie,
Making faces in mirrors and asking me why.

Layers of laughter pile high on the shelf,
As I inspect the landscape, I chuckle myself.
Oh, the paths that I wander, the trails I explore,
In the mosaic of me, there's always room for more.

So let's toast to the funny in each dappled hue,
To the quirks and the laughs that make life feel new.
In a world painted silly, we find a way through,
A mosaic of moments adorned just for you.

Where Shadows Hold Their Secrets

In the corner, a shadow silently sits,
It whispers my secrets, and oh, what fits!
With a grin, it wiggles and dances so sly,
Spilling the beans with a wink and a sigh.

I search for the truth in its playful disguise,
But all that I find are its humorous lies.
It chuckles and tumbles with glee up and down,
Where shadows are jesters, and laughter's the crown.

Each flicker of light draws a comic delight,
As shadows perform in a whimsical night.
They share all my blunders, my trips on the way,
Turn failures to funny, in shadows they play.

So here's to the mysteries that darkness can weave,
In the giggles of whispers, I choose to believe.
Where shadows are keepers of jokes yet untold,
In this playful dimension, life's secrets unfold.

Gazing into the Mirror of Time

I gaze in the glass and my past waves hello,
With a face full of giggles and hairstyles of yow!
Time takes a snapshot, then pulls a sly prank,
Making me chuckle at the things I once drank.

Reflections of choices, both wise and absurd,
Where I wrangled with fortunes, and laughter occurred.
In each wrinkle and laugh line, history sings,
Of days filled with chaos and odd little things.

I ponder the years, like a pie gone awry,
Each slice tells a story, some flavor to try.
I raise a toast to the hiccups and glee,
In the front row of time, I'm just happy to be.

So let's dance with reflections, a whimsical ride,
The mirror's a friend where my chuckles abide.
In the theater of life, let the laughs always chime,
For every old wrinkle tells tales rich in time.

Tracing Footsteps in Memory's Soil

In the garden of my mind,
Old paths of laughter unwind.
Chasing shadows of lost days,
With each step, my memory sways.

Potatoes whisper, 'Dig a hole!'
While carrots dance, they play the role.
I trip on daisies, what a sight,
These roots of joy, oh what delight!

Slip on puddles, splatter and spritz,
Nostalgia's game can be a blitz.
Running in circles, I lose my shoe,
Yet every fall brings laughter too.

Beneath the smiles that I recall,
Lie moments that may yet enthrall.
With a wink, the past comes out to play,
In this silly dance, I'll forever stay.

A Tapestry of Inner Whispers

In the fabric of my thoughts,
Like tangled yarn, each lesson knots.
Threads of giggles, some of woe,
Weaving in place, oh what a show!

Laughter stitches, tears unravel,
In this maze, I takes my travel.
A snail slips by with a cheeky grin,
Waving his shell, he invites me in.

Whispers echo through the seams,
Tickling my brain, igniting dreams.
One sock is lost, a shoe is found,
In the chaos, joy is abound.

With mismatched patterns, I shall dance,
To the rhythm of my silly prance.
Embracing the quirks of my mind's tale,
In this tapestry, I shall prevail.

The Garden of Forgotten Dreams

In a plot where daydreams sleep,
Beneath the daisies, memories creep.
A pumpkin sighs, "Don't let me rot!"
While spinach giggles, 'What a plot!'

Swinging on vines, I lost my way,
Chased by the breeze on a sunny day.
A scarecrow with a crooked smile,
Winks at me from the row, "Stay awhile!"

Mismatched seeds in the ground I toss,
Hoping to grow my thoughts across.
With every sprout, a tale appears,
In this wild garden, I shed my fears.

Among the weeds, I find my zest,
In forgotten dreams, I'm truly blessed.
With laughter growing, as flowers do,
This garden's bloom is just for you.

When Time Pauses for Thought

Tick-tock, the clock takes a break,
As I ponder, it's no mistake.
Spilled coffee on my favorite chair,
Laughing as I give it a stare.

Seconds linger, they start to dance,
While I trip over my second glance.
A cat meows, 'Hey, where's the fun?'
Time's playing hide-and-seek, just run!

In this stillness, my mind wanders,
Chasing after all my blunders.
I trip on truths, and tumble deep,
While silly secrets begin to leap.

Yet in this pause, I find a thrill,
Each chuckle fuels my heart to fill.
So here I sit, with giggles in sight,
When time takes a breath, everything's right.

Diving Deep into Still Waters

In the pond, I take a leap,
My splash wakes frogs from sleep.
Fish swim by with knowing grins,
As I ponder my silly sins.

Bubbles rise, thoughts float away,
Drowning in mirth is my play.
Water's calm, yet my mind's a whirl,
Who knew thoughts could dance and twirl?

Plumbing depths for pearls of jest,
Each flub a hidden fest.
What treasures lie beneath this calm?
Just laughter, like a soothing balm.

With a twist, I dive anew,
Bringing back the silliest view.
At the surface, I gasp and grin,
Still waters laugh at a tale within.

The Weight of Unspoken Thoughts

I've a brain, yet feel like lead,
Thoughts ballooned, can't say a word!
Ideas piled, like laundry stacks,
Heavy weight with no relaxing hacks.

Every glance feels like a weight,
Underneath my poker face, fate.
I'd speak more if I could unseal,
This hodgepodge of ideas concealed.

A pigeon lands atop my brain,
It coos and wiggles, feels insane!
What if I let a thought slip free?
I wonder if they'd laugh at me?

Next time I'll try a belly laugh,
Instead of thinking, do the math!
A twist of fate, or cosmic jest,
Unspoken words take a funny rest.

Unfolding Layers of the Self

I peel back layers, like an onion,
What's beneath? A clown or a ton?
Each tear falls, laughter rings clear,
Finding humor in what's so dear.

A tangle of socks, oh the mess,
These layers, I must confess!
My thoughts are hiding in the fold,
Behind fabric stories, bold and old.

I'm a burrito of silly dreams,
Wrapped tight in my quirky schemes.
With every layer peeled away,
I giggle at what I've kept at bay.

Perhaps I'll find a rubber chicken,
Or a treasure trove of joy just kickin'.
A layered laugh, deep and wide,
Shows the funny self I can't hide.

Echoes Beneath the Bark

Trees sway and whisper in the breeze,
Do they chuckle at birds and bees?
With every rustle, a giggle erupts,
As branches wiggle, they laugh uncut.

Below the bark, secrets abound,
Riddles of nature go round and round.
Roots tap dance beneath the ground,
Each echo revealing what's profound.

I stand and listen, ear to the tree,
Hoping its laughter spills over me.
But all I hear are silly quips,
Between squirrels and their acorn trips.

Nature's humor, a riot of fun,
With echoes of life, a cosmic pun.
I chuckle with trees, in total glee,
As the world joins in this playful spree.

The Mirror's Embrace

In the glass, my hair's a mess,
It yells, 'Why not wear a dress?'
I smile wide, that grin's a fight,
With morning coffee, it's all alright.

But when I dance, my feet go fly,
The mirror laughs, I wonder why?
Reflecting back a jester's face,
In this chaotic, silly space.

I strike a pose, but then I trip,
The mirror mocks my funny slip.
But in its depths, I find a mate,
In joy and laughter, I create.

So here's to me, the quirky king,
In every gaffe, a joyful fling.
The mirror and I share a joke,
As we both giggle and provoke.

Silent Conversations

In the corner sits my old chair,
We chat for hours, nobody's there.
It squeaks a lot, so I agree,
That it's a bit more wise than me.

With every creak, it tells a tale,
Of clumsy trips and food that fails.
We snicker at the crumbs we dropped,
In silent talks, the best thoughts cropped.

I pour my tea and spill it wide,
The chair just chuckles, takes its stride.
It knows my woes, my highs, my lows,
An armchair friend when laughter flows.

In this duet of thoughts and cheer,
I find a comfort, loud and clear.
For every secret, every dream,
My chair and I, a perfect team.

Harvesting Memories

With a basket full of chuckles bright,
I gather feelings, take my flight.
Each laugh like apples, ripe and sweet,
Mingling joy with every treat.

I pluck the moments, one by one,
When silly thoughts spark just for fun.
Like tomatoes that squirt on a dare,
Each memory shines, without a care.

In the garden where I plant my doubt,
I pull the weeds and scream out loud.
As laughter blooms amid the greens,
I harvest joy, forget the means.

At twilight's door, I stroll back home,
With giggles gathered, that's my poem.
Each funny tale a seed I sow,
In the harvest where bright memories grow.

Ties That Ground Us

In tangled wires and lines we find,
Connections deep, yet undefined.
A mix of laughter, jokes, and ties,
That keep us close, beneath the skies.

With every hug, we wrangle tight,
Like plants that twist in morning light.
Each silly story, a branch that sways,
A bond that grows through all our days.

Through ups and downs, we dance around,
In goofy steps, our hearts unbound.
With every trip and silly fall,
We tie our hearts, we hear the call.

So here we stand, with laughter free,
In every moment, joy's decree.
For in the fun, we surely see,
The threads that weave this tapestry.

Finding Clarity in the Quiet

In silence, thoughts begin to play,
Whispers of wisdom in a dance,
But every time I drift away,
I trip on socks left at a glance.

Laughter echoes down the halls,
As echoes bounce like rubber balls,
I ponder life while on the loo,
Sipping tea and feeling blue.

My mind's a maze, a twisty thing,
In polite company, I might sing,
But all they hear are awkward sighs,
And muffled giggles; oh, what a prize!

In quiet's grip, the truth unfolds,
Like dirt in gardens, rich and bold,
I strut about, with flair and glee,
Who knew reflection could be free?

Time Enshrined in Gentle Reflection

Tick-tock whispers on the wall,
Remind me not to trip and fall,
In grand design, my thoughts entwine,
While ducks in ponds form a straight line.

The clock keeps ticking, what a chore,
While my mind wanders out the door,
Just like my socks—missing, it seems,
Where do they go? Oh, lost in dreams!

I sit with coffee, pondering fate,
Of burnt toast and lunch on a plate,
As I zone out, my thoughts conspire,
To roast a marshmallow on a wire.

Yet here I sit, with laughter meek,
With muse who's stubborn and quite bleak,
In this dance of seconds, I find the fun,
As reality spins and life's a pun!

The Garden Path of Contemplation

I stroll along my garden path,
Observing weeds, doing the math,
These wildflowers wear a crown,
While I wear slippers, kind of brown.

My thoughts take flight like wayward bees,
Buzzing 'round with all the ease,
But instead of nectar, I seek a snack,
Oh look, a squirrel—hey, come back!

In the dirt, a thought takes root,
Like carrots hiding, shy and cute,
I laugh at worms beneath my feet,
Trying to dance, oh, quite the feat!

A chuckle spills from lips so wide,
As I ponder what life's supplied,
In this garden, wackiness blooms,
And joy wafts through like sweet perfumes.

Embracing the Stillness of Being

In stillness, I embrace my chair,
Cushions hugging, dreams in the air,
But wait! The cat jumps on my knee,
And purrs a tune, so off-key!

With coffee splashed on yesterday's news,
I contemplate the world's odd views,
Is time a trickster with a wink?
Or am I just a thing that blinks?

As moments twirl with comic flair,
Like dancing through a grizzly bear,
I chuckle soft, with pillows stuffed,
Not knowing if I've just had enough!

So here I sit, with zen in mind,
Unraveling silliness, blissfully blind,
In stillness, life's peculiar jive,
Reflecting laughs, oh how I thrive!

Reflection in a Puddle of Time

I peered into a puddle deep,
Saw my frown and thought, "No sleep!"
A frog jumped in, said, "What a mess!"
"Your hair is wild, your pants, I guess!"

Time drips slow like honey's flow,
Why do I hurry? I don't quite know.
Each wrinkle shared a tale of glee,
At least my shoes are shiny, me!

My thoughts bounce 'round like rubber balls,
In endless echoes of restroom stalls.
What if I wore socks, not shoes?
Would the world just laugh, or call me 'moose'?

So here I stand, a woeful clown,
With dreams of a glowing, grand renown.
But as I gaze, the frog just croaks,
"Your life's a show—it's full of jokes!"

Embrace the splashes, laugh with grace,
Look in that puddle, it's not a race.
With every smile, we find a rhyme,
Amidst the chaos of puddles and time.

The Depths of Quiet Contemplation

In silence deep, I stroke my chin,
Too much quiet? Where do I begin?
A thought pops up like toast from bread,
"Is that my hair or what's in my head?"

Birds outside squawk their wild plans,
While I sip coffee in fuzzy pants.
Reflecting on deep cosmic things,
Like why my phone still needs new rings.

A cat curls up, looks wise and fat,
I ask, "Are you pondering like that?"
It yawns back, glances towards the sun,
"Hey buddy, chilling's really fun!"

So I toss thoughts like paper planes,
Through the depths of my quirky brain.
And as I sit in cozy confusion,
I realize life's a funny illusion.

Seeds of Wisdom in the Dark

In the dark, I plant my dreams,
Hoping they bloom with silly themes.
A wisdom seed, what a strange crop,
Next to my shoes, they both may flop!

Tried to dig deep, but hit my toe,
Funny how wisdom can often go slow.
An acorn said, "Hey, plant me right!"
I laughed, said, "You've got jokes tonight!"

And so I water my quirky sprouts,
With cups of coffee and lots of doubts.
If they grow tall, will I look sweet?
Or just a nut, dodging my own feet?

But in the dark, let laughter sprout,
Because clowning around is what it's about.
So here's to seeds that don't quite grow,
In the dark, we make quite a show!

Shadows of the Soul's Landscape

My shadows dance in the twilight glow,
They mimic my moves, put on a show.
With every step, a pirouette,
"Hey dude, is that an awkward pet?"

A squirrel scolds, "Your shadow's a mess!"
"At least it has no laundry stress!"
We giggle and groan on this wobbly stage,
Life's just a script, with an odd page.

I trip on thoughts that like to tease,
Like socks on hands or mismatched knees.
The sun sets low, painting the sky,
While shadows chuckle at passersby.

So let's waltz on through this jolly plight,
With flappy shoulders and hearts so light.
In the shadows, we find our play,
Laughing together till the end of day.

Where Time Stands Still

In a clock shop where seconds snooze,
Tick-tock turtles sip on their brews.
A grumpy old watch gives a great big yawn,
While hourglasses nap, all the sand is withdrawn.

The cuckoo's gone out for a long, long break,
His call now a whisper, a feathery ache.
I wonder who runs the minutes in here,
Maybe a squirrel, or a wise old deer?

The calendar's stuck; it's perpetually June,
With tighty whiteys hanging under the moon.
So I'm waltzing with clocks, in this comical swirl,
Where time's just a concept, like a dance with a girl.

So if you find time traveling, just watch your step,
For laughing at logic could lead to a rep.
In this timeless abyss, where giggles fulfill,
Let's embrace all that's quirky, where time stands still.

Thoughts Drifting on a Gentle Breeze

A thought floats by on a butterfly wing,
Wearing a hat made of tinsel and bling.
It giggles and winks, 'Come join in my race!'
But I'm stuck in my chair, with crumbs on my face.

The clouds are quite chubby, like marshmallows fluff,
As they gossiped of rain, which sounded quite tough.
"Are you bummed?" whispered wind, with a cheeky grin,
"Grab an umbrella, let's twirl in the din!"

Dancing through daisies, my mind takes a whirl,
Spinning like tops, with a twist and a twirl.
Each thought a balloon, drifting high in the air,
Chasing a giggle, like it's not even rare.

So let's gather our laughter, my whimsical friends,
And see where this journey of daydreams descends.
For the breeze has a knack of making us free,
With thoughts drifting lightly, quite humorously.

Pieces of Time in Quietude

In a library thick with dust bunnies' thrill,
I found missing socks, time stood very still.
An old man with glasses said, "Grab a chair!"
As he scribbled on napkins without a single care.

Pages are turning, like the wheel of a bike,
With whispers of stories that giggle and strike.
The clock on the wall, it tilts at a glance,
While the cat in the corner, is plotting romance.

Teacups are chatting, "Oh, what a fine day,
To spill all our secrets in this quirky café!"
And the sunlight unravels, like yarn from a ball,
While we laugh with the shadows playing games on the wall.

In this bizarre haven where silence can tease,
A chuckle erupts with the buzz of the bees.
So let's take these pieces, this droll interlude,
And weave them together, our oddness renewed.

Mapping the Traces of the Past

With a pencil and paper, I track down a clue,
Footprints in custard; oh, what a stew!
The paths that I wander, they giggle and sway,
In a world that's absurd, come join my ballet.

Finding old socks with a laughter-filled spark,
They dance on the timeline, quite quirky and dark.
Map out where I tripped on the green gooey grass,
While it tickles my toes—how long will it last?

Maps drawn in frosting, with sprinkles galore,
Lead me to places I've never been before.
A fork in the road? I'll take them all, please!
With a slice of good humor and such tasty ease.

So let's draw our maps with giggles and cheer,
For the traces we follow hold laughter so dear.
Each pickle and prance tells a story so vast,
In this whimsical journey, we're mapping the past.

Wisps of Sentiment in Still Air

In the breeze, a thought takes flight,
Wiggling like a worm in broad daylight.
Chasing shadows, giggling loud,
As whispers form a lively crowd.

Echoes of laughter shake the trees,
Searching for sanity, but finding cheese.
The clouds wear hats, quite absurd,
While squirrels audition for the birdword.

Bouncing ideas, like silly springs,
Tangled up in what nonsense brings.
A breeze, a giggle, a thought awry,
In stillness, I can't help but fly.

Sit back, relax, let mind unwind,
In a realm where crazy's kind.
A thought garden where jesters play,
Embracing the night, while sparrows sway.

In the Garden of Inner Thoughts

In a patch of daisies, I trip on my brain,
Dodging a butterfly, swatting at rain.
A carrot debates with a wise old beet,
As laughter erupts from my silly feet.

Weeds of worry try to intrude,
Yet petals of joy are the finest food.
Each squiggle and wiggle, a dance of the mind,
Growing ideas of the funniest kind.

Garden gnomes gossip behind sneaky flowers,
Plotting the best of their trivial powers.
With a pop and a giggle, they jump all around,
Harmless chaos is surely profound.

Let rainbows dissolve into pieces of pie,
While fireflies hum nonsensical why.
In this inner garden, a jester's delight,
Where the weeds wear boots and the sun shines bright.

The Soundtrack of Solitude

In still spaces, the silence hums,
Like a fridge that's lost its sense of drums.
A symphony of crickets playing sour,
While thoughts tango in an unshowered hour.

Echoes of yawn meet daydream groans,
The radio spills out its forgotten tones.
Distant chuckles fill the air,
As my sock drawer shares its quirky flair.

A clock tickles as it skips a beat,
While chairs make chatter with all their creaks.
In solitude, a wild boogie grows,
As I join in, striking ridiculous poses.

The cat joins in with a dubious stare,
While I trip over dreams, tangled in air.
In this one-man show, a raucous play,
Who knew being alone brought such a display?

Leaves Falling into Still Moments

Autumn leaves, a tumble of thoughts,
Dancing around with dapper knots.
Each twist and turn, a snicker or tease,
As squirrels debate the virtues of cheese.

Each leaf a giggle, a flutter, a sigh,
Whispering secrets that bounce and fly.
A laugh echoes softly down the lane,
While pumpkins roll around, playing coy in the rain.

As branches chuckle, the ground gives a cheer,
The wind bursts in, picking up gear.
In this choir of oddities, I find my place,
Dancing with shadows, a comical chase.

Embracing the whimsy of moments that pass,
As the world spins laughter, with a wink and a glass.
In stillness, I join this merry parade,
Where joy is the music, and silly is played.

The Unfolding Scroll of the Past

In a dusty tome, the past does hide,
With secrets that giggle, they cannot abide.
Old sock puppets dance, they tell funny tales,
Of a cat in a hat who rode on a whale.

Each line a rubber band, stretched out with glee,
Ticklish memories, caught like a bee.
With every twist, another laugh spills,
As time tickles me gently, with all of its thrills.

Oh, what a ruckus, our yesterdays play,
Mismatched socks waltzing at the end of the day.
The goblins in closets, they chuckle and cheer,
For yesterday's antics are always so near.

So let us unravel this scroll of delight,
With misadventures that take flight at night.
For amidst all the lessons, a giggle we find,
In the silly old stories that linger behind.

A Reverie Amongst Shadows

In corners where shadows like secrets do creep,
A memory tickles, it starts with a leap.
An old rubber chicken just won't accept,
That the stories we tell are the ones we forget.

The shadows do prance, they whisper out loud,
Of a banana peel slip, oh, how it was bowed!
With giggles and gasps, we'd slip in a race,
And fumble amidst socks, oh, the laughs on our face.

They sway in the night like a dance on the wall,
Us chuckling softly at those moments of fall.
So let's dive into darkness where laughter takes flight,
And paint all our shadows with humor and light.

In fleeting reflections, amidst dark and bright,
The past makes us chuckle, oh what a sight!
For even our quirks, like the moon up above,
Are spun into stories of laughter and love.

Reflections in the Silence

In silence, a mirror starts winking at me,
Its shimmers do giggle, oh what could it be?
A silent old parrot, with one eye in jest,
Repeats all the secrets we thought were the best.

Quiet chuckles slip through the cracks of the day,
As reflections pretend that they'll lead us astray.
With whispers of hiccups and snickers of yore,
The quietest giggles are the loudest encore.

A pondering cat with the gift of a grin,
Witty observations of all we've been in.
As echoes roll softly, with cheeky delight,
It's the quietest moments that make laughter ignite.

So here in this silence, let joy be the guide,
With reflections that twinkle, we'll laugh and abide.
For amidst all the whispers and muted refrain,
Are stories that trickle with laughter again.

Dances of Memory in Dappled Light

In sunlight's embrace, the memories prance,
Like daisies in bloom, they twist in a dance.
Each glimmering moment's a wiggle and jig,
A remembered mishap, a hop and a gig.

They flutter and flop, like a fish on dry land,
Silly misadventures that go hand in hand.
As dappled light dapples, our past does deploy,
The whirls of our laughter, the bounce of our joy.

A twirl in the grass with a splash of bright hue,
Each dance tells a story, a chuckle or two.
With toes tapping lightly, we spin through the air,
For memories wrapped up in giggles declare.

So let's dance through our days, in the warm sunlight,
Where laughter's a compass, the world feels just right.
With each step we take, in this whimsical flight,
We stamp on the echoes of joy, pure and bright.

Nature's Quiet Lament

In the woods, the trees do sigh,
They gossip softly, oh my, oh my!
A leaf fell down, like a clumsy ballet,
Nature giggles, what a funny display!

The brook babbles secrets so slick,
Wishing for a rock to do the trick.
A frog croaks jokes, straight from the pond,
Even the crickets have a band they're fond!

The squirrel plots, on the highest limb,
To steal the acorns, it's all on a whim.
But the nut he wants rolls far away,
It's a game of chase, nature's own play!

A flower blushes in morning's light,
But a bee's bad aim gave her a fright.
In every laugh, the world seems alive,
In nature's theater, we all can thrive!

Anchored in Silence

In a quiet corner, a snail sets sail,
Saying, "I'm late, but I'll leave a trail!"
The wind whooshes by with a chuckle,
While the trees attempt to do a huddle.

A stone sits heavy, with tales to tell,
Of wandering feet that tripped and fell.
He grins and waits for a toe to stub,
Nature's old jokester, a true little bub!

The clouds float by, like fluffy sheep,
Boarding on laughter, secrets to keep.
Raindrops giggle when they hit the ground,
Making puddles where giggles abound!

The silence, it hums in a quirky tune,
As shadows pirouette beneath the moon.
In the stillness, there's always a jest,
Even the crickets know laughter is best!

Beneath the Canopy of Time

A wise old oak wears a wrinkled face,
He chuckles softly at the squirrel race.
Time tickles leaves, still shaking the dust,
"Hold on," he whispers, "in laughter we trust!"

A nimble rabbit hops to and fro,
With a hat on his head, stealing the show.
The fox rolls his eyes, "Is he for real?"
Nature's own circus, with farcical feel!

As shadows dance under the leafy dome,
Each twig tells a story, a tiny poem.
And the breeze plays tricks, pulling hair and hats,
While birds crack wise like they've seen all the spats!

Mossy green laughter spreads wide and far,
In this moment, we all are a star.
Under time's watch, life's antics amuse,
With chuckles and cheers, what more can you choose?

Footprints of the Soul

Tiny footprints in the sand so light,
Each one giggles at the seagull's flight.
"Hey there, bird, you think you can sing?"
The waves crash back, "Oh, what joy you bring!"

A turtle stumbles, but wears a grin,
While starfish do cartwheels, with a spin!
The beach is a stage for the waves to play,
Crafting new tales in a salty ballet!

Footprints dancing, skip and sway,
"Mistaken identity!" the crab will say.
With every step, laughter fills the air,
A cosmic joke, forever we share!

So wander the shores with playful cheer,
And let the sea sing softly in your ear.
In life's myriad footprints, let's leave a trace,
Of giggles and joy, in this vast, open space!

Silent Growth Amidst Chaos

In a world where noise reigns supreme,
The plants just sigh and plot their dream.
With roots so deep, they stand their ground,
While chaos swirls all around.

A daisy laughs at a passing dog,
While sprouts engage in a morning jog.
They whisper secrets to the breeze,
As squirrels race up with such great ease.

Beneath the chaos, there's a dance,
Each leaf and stem takes a chance.
In the garden, the veggies play,
Chasing sunlight during the day.

And when the storm sends thunders' groan,
They huddle close, not alone.
With roots so strong, they'll never sway,
In laughter, they bloom through disarray.

Whispers of Silent Memories

In the quiet, whispers float,
Of memories on a tiny boat.
The tomatoes giggle at their past,
While memories in sunlight cast.

Old carrots share tales of their youth,
With beets who claim they tell the truth.
The spinach dreams of long-lost days,
And dances in the sun's warm rays.

With every thought, a chuckle grows,
As daisies ponder how time flows.
Each petal holds a silly tale,
Of bees who think they're quite the whale.

In silent laughter, they all bloom,
Creating joy amidst the gloom.
So let us sit and share a laugh,
With nature's finest autograph.

Beneath the Surface of Thought

Beneath the soil, a party brews,
With radishes sporting colorful hues.
They wiggle roots in joyful cheer,
Creating fun without a fear.

Thoughts like worms twist and twirl,
In the dark, they take a whirl.
With every idea, a giggle sprouts,
As laughter dances all about.

Beneath the surface, whispers play,
A secret world that loves the day.
The fungi join in, wearing hats,
And sing of joys with tiny bats.

So let your thoughts take a trip,
In this garden, give laughter a flip.
For fun and growth go hand in hand,
In a whimsical, wacky land.

Echoes of the Mind's Garden

In the garden where thoughts collide,
Echoes giggle and dance with pride.
Each plant's a thought, sprouting high,
While clouds above just float and sigh.

The flowers trade tales, flower by flower,
Of that time when they sprouted power.
With laughter laced in every seed,
They dance around, fulfilling a need.

In the air, a breeze of mirth,
Whispers of wisdom, and light rebirth.
The vegetables plot a comedy show,
While herbs in the back row gently glow.

With every echo, the garden thrives,
In this laughter, the spirit derives.
So join the fun, let your thoughts grow,
In this garden of joy, let your grin show.

Soft Murmurs in the Back of the Mind

In a cozy nook of thought so tight,
A squirrel chuckles at a crazy sight.
Lost keys dance in a jazzy parade,
While my brain's on a lunch break, pretty swayed.

Thoughts drift by like clouds in the air,
One wears a tutu, what a funny flair!
Nostalgia's giggle whispers my name,
As I trip over memories sans any shame.

A pizza slice sings songs of the past,
With pepperoni dreams growing absurdly vast.
My brain's like a circus, full of delight,
Where clowns in my noggin are taking flight.

So here's to the whispers we try to ignore,
The silly ideas that leave us wanting more.
In the depths of my mind, there's always a grin,
Chasing these musings is where the fun begins.

In the Stillness of the Heart

Between beats, a jolly joke does reside,
A tickle of laughter I can't seem to hide.
An echoing chuckle from deep down below,
Like a rubber chicken, it's ready to show.

In quiet moments, silly thoughts play tag,
While ice cream cones wear wigs, oh what a brag!
My heart's a dance floor, with rhythms so sweet,
A polka-dotted bunny shuffles its feet.

Whispers of love act like clowns on parade,
With every reflection, a joke's serenade.
So let's giggle together, my dear, hold tight,
In the stillness of hearts, let's laugh through the night.

When shadows waltz and the stars start to peek,
A tickle of hope makes my chuckles unique.
For in quietude's corner lies joy that ignites,
Transforming the stillness into playful delights.

Beneath the Canopy of the Past

Under the shade of memories' trees,
A raccoon juggles to entertain the bees.
Epic stories of socks lost in the wash,
Whisper through branches with a whimsical swash.

Once upon a time, when I wore mismatched shoes,
The universe chuckled and offered me clues.
Beneath ancient blooms, the past likes to sway,
As I try to remember where I left my bouquet.

In laughter's embrace, I find colors so bright,
Like rainbows that giggle beneath the moonlight.
The roots of my foolishness sink deep in the ground,
Where echoes of laughter are happily found.

With every glance back, a smile takes flight,
As the past throws confetti and parties all night.
So I dance through the memories, with glee on my face,
In the canopy's laughter, I've found my place.

The Echoes of What Was

In the abyss of echoes, a tune softly plays,
A melody muddied by yesterday's haze.
A duet of goofiness sings out loud,
As the ghosts of my choices gather in a crowd.

The pizza box laughs from its throne on the shelf,
Revisiting moments, a time-traveling elf.
Every blunder reflects like a disco ball,
Spinning old tales that make me enthrall.

Socks turned to puppets crack jokes without fail,
While clocks giggle softly, a tick-tocky tale.
The echoes of what was keep bouncing around,
Adding humor to wisdom, in silliness found.

So let's toast to our follies, those whimsical flops,
For in laughter's embrace, nobody stops.
As echoes resound, may we bring forth a cheer,
To the stories that linger, forever sincere.

Notes from the Echo Chamber of the Soul

In the hall of thoughts, I hear a shout,
A voice so loud, I wonder how it got out.
It echoes here like a bouncing ball,
Is it wisdom or just the fridge's call?

I scribble notes on napkins and walls,
Trying to catch what the echo recalls.
It laughs and giggles, a real prankster,
As I ponder hard like a jester's dancer.

My brain's a circus, the clowns parade,
Each thought a stunt, some brilliantly played.
Yet sometimes the lion is all that I see,
Roaring back with questions: "Who else thinks like me?"

So here I sit, with my echo so grand,
A symphony of thoughts, none quite as planned.
I raise a toast to this raucous crew,
For without their noise, I'd have nothing to do!

In the Depths of Thoughtful Solitude

In my solitude, I find some friends,
Like dust bunnies that won't meet their ends.
They weave and twirl like a funky dance,
No chance of escape, I give them a glance.

Thoughts bubble up like a soda pop,
Some fizz so loud, they make my head bop.
I laugh at the ideas that come out to play,
Like socks on my feet when I'm all out of sway.

Each giggle I catch is a treasure to hold,
A joke made of silver with glittering gold.
I tickle my brain, give it some flair,
Only to find there's few with whom to share.

Yet here I sit, in my quiet retreat,
Digging for laughter beneath my own seat.
The silence is thick but humor's the theme,
In my world of one, I'm living the dream!

Memory's Canvas in Soft Hues

I paint my memories in pastel light,
With crayons of joy and a sprinkle of fright.
Erasers in hand, I change my past,
Making mistakes come out a blast!

The canvas is stretched, but oh what a scene,
With dancing cats where the grass should be green.
In shades of laughter, I scribble and swoosh,
Creating a masterpiece, calls for a whoosh!

Some colors collide, a riotous mix,
Like marshmallows tossed in risky old tricks.
And though the picture's a bit out of line,
It's a whimsical wonder, this art of mine.

So here's to the hues that brighten my day,
In a world of chaos, I paint my own way.
For every laugh's a stroke of the brush,
In memory's gallery, I always get a rush!

The Stories Written in Silence

In silent halls, stories start to creep,
Whispers of secrets, too shy to leap.
They trip on their tongues and tumble right down,
Painting my mind with a comical frown.

I watch as the silence begins to chat,
About the lost keys and my missing hat.
Each tale is a giggle, stifled and small,
Waiting for echo to bounce off the wall.

The shadows converse, plotting their fun,
As I twist and turn, dodging surf and sun.
With each silent giggle, an audible space,
The laughter erupts, it's a riot to face!

So here I'll remain, in this quiet delight,
Collecting the stories that flutter in flight.
In the realm of silence, the humor's no myth,
For the loudest of tales come without any gift!

www.ingramcontent.com/pod-product-compliance
Lightning Source LLC
Chambersburg PA
CBHW072214070526
44585CB00015B/1341